VIOLIN PLAY-ALONG

AUDIO ACCESS INCLUDED

TAYLOR DAVIS FAVORITES

VOL. 73

PLAYBACK+
Speed • Pitch • Balance • Loop

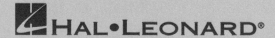

To access audio visit:
www.halleonard.com/mylibrary

1179-3476-5450-0952

ISBN 978-1-5400-1527-3

Cover photo by Aga Jones Photography

Transcribed by Jonathan T. Mathews

Jon Vriesacker, violin
Audio arrangements by Peter Deneff
Recorded and Produced by Jake Johnson
at Paradyme Productions

HAL•LEONARD®

Visit Hal Leonard Online at
www.halleonard.com

Contact Us:
Hal Leonard
7777 West Bluemound Road
Milwaukee, WI 53213
Email: info@halleonard.com

In Europe contact:
Hal Leonard Europe Limited
42 Wigmore Street
Marylebone, London, W1U 2RN
Email: info@halleonardeurope.com

In Australia contact:
Hal Leonard Australia Pty. Ltd.
4 Lentara Court
Cheltenham, Victoria, 3192 Australia
Email: info@halleonard.com.au

Bratja
(Brothers)
from FULL METAL ALCHEMIST

Words and Music by Michiru Oshima, Seiji Mizushima and Tatiana Naumova
Arranged by Taylor Davis

Concerning Hobbits

from THE LORD OF THE RINGS: THE FELLOWSHIP OF THE RING
By Howard Shore
Arranged by Taylor Davis and Adam Gubman

For the Love of a Princess

from the Twentieth Century Fox Motion Picture BRAVEHEART
Music by James Horner
Arranged by Taylor Davis and Adam Gubman

Guren-No-Yumiya
(Attack On Titan)

By Revo
Arranged by Taylor Davis and Adam Gubman

Megalovania

from UNDERTALE®
Music by Toby Fox
Arranged by Taylor Davis

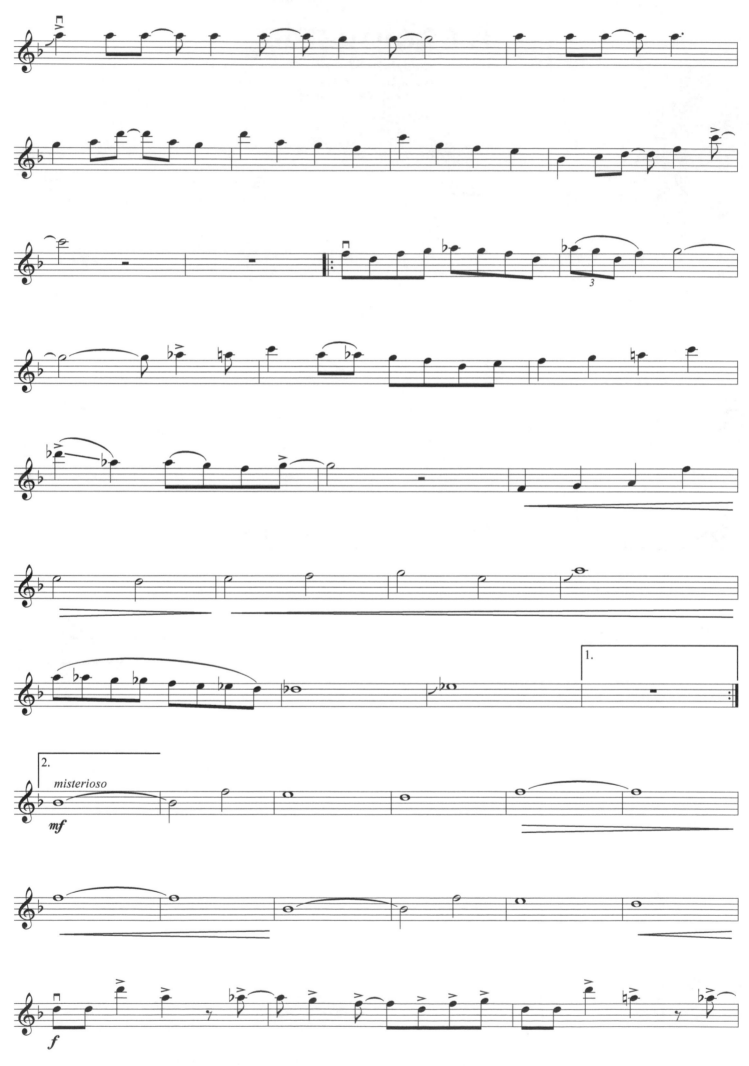

14

scherzando

cresc.

ff

Hedwig's Theme

from the Motion Picture HARRY POTTER AND THE SORCERER'S STONE
Music by John Williams
Arranged by Taylor Davis and Adam Gubman

Swordland to Be Continued

from SWORD ART ONLINE
By Yuki Kajiura
Arranged by Taylor Davis

Now We Are Free

from the DreamWorks film GLADIATOR

Written by Hans Zimmer, Lisa Gerrard and Klaus Badelt
Arranged by Taylor Davis and Adam Gubman